A Stoic's Guide to Social Media

Navigating Online Chaos

Table of Contents

Chapter 1. Introduction

In our special report, "A Stoic's Guide to Social Media: Navigating Online Chaos," we delve deep into the crevices of the virtual world to equip you with the right mental tools to surf the internet waves with peace and composure. This isn't about algorithms, coding, or machine learning; it's about the human element of our online interactions. With a touch of the ancient philosophy of Stoicism, often embraced by the wisest of minds, this guide is here to revitalize your approach to social media and fortify your mental resilience. Imagine sunlit tranquility amidst a storm of tweets, posts, comments, and shares—this could be your daily reality. Don't just survive the digital age, thrive in it. Get ready to embark on a transformative journey that promises excitement and steadiness in equal measure. Tempted? You should be! Open the door to a healthier, happier virtual life with our report today!

Chapter 2. Introducing Stoicism: A Brief Overview

The philosophy of Stoicism, born in the tumult of ancient Greece, offers a timeless toolkit for not only combating our modern digital anxieties but strengthening our resilience to them. Articulated by the likes of Epictetus, Seneca, and Marcus Aurelius, these early Stoics have left us a trove of wisdom relevant to our media-infused lives. Let's dive into this philosophical system that can help us make sense of our interconnected, digital world, providing a salve to the furor of social media.

2.1. Stoicism: The Birth

Stoicism was born in Athens in the early 3rd century BCE, and it was then nurtured in the hands of thinkers like Zeno of Citium, Cleanthes, and Chrysippus. It was coined with the name 'Stoicism' due to the Stoa Poikile location in Athens, wherein Zeno, its founder, would often hold his philosophical teachings—Stoa meaning 'porch.'

The Stoics held a profound and holistic vision of life, encompassing logic, ethics, and understanding nature. While the Stoic philosopher might delve into questions about perception, inference, or paradoxes, their efforts were always guided by their commitment to leading virtuous lives.

2.2. Virtue is the Sole Good

"Virtue is the sole good," declared the Stoics, a statement carrying an intrinsic sense of simplicity and profundity. This was not a blind belief but rather an insight. For them, everything we need to lead a good, fulfilled life is already within us. It's about performing one's duties, being socially responsible, maintaining rationality against emotional disturbances, and accepting whatever life throws at us with equanimity.

Stoics saw emotions as the result of judgment, and by training ourselves, refining our judgments, we could achieve what they called 'apatheia,' which stood for peace of mind. This does not mean living a life devoid of all emotions, but rather achieving a state of tranquillity where we are no longer overwhelmed by them.

2.3. Understanding Stoic Ethics

Stoic ethics, with their cornerstone in virtue, are established on four cardinal virtues: wisdom (sophia), courage (andreia), justice (dikaiosyne), and moderation (sophrosyne). Wisdom denotes understanding life as it is; courage refers to being brave in tough times; justice means behaving with fairness and kindness; and moderation stands for self-control.

These virtues were seen as interconnected and inseparable. Wisdom was not just intellectual understanding, but wisdom in action, prompting justice, courage, and moderation. To be virtuous meant to act according to rational nature, living in harmony with oneself and the world.

2.4. Examining Stoic Physics

Though it might seem far from our exploration of social media, Stoic physics, the understanding of the natural world, plays a crucial role in fortifying our state of mind. For Stoics, the universe was a rational entity guided by Logos, a cosmic reason or divine principle, allowing them to accept life events as they unfolded, viewing them as part of nature's course.

The Stoic dogma 'Amor Fati,' accepting and loving one's fate, embodies this worldview—treating each event, success or failure, as a necessary part of the universe's rational unfolding. This perspective helps develop resilience, a mental strength that is incredibly useful in navigating the tumultuous world of social media.

2.5. Stoicism and Death

Death was not a taboo for Stoics but a subject of deep contemplation. Marcus Aurelius wrote extensively on the matter, viewing it as a natural part of life and not something to be feared. This attitude towards mortality led them towards memento mori, the practice of reflecting on mortality to live a more meaningful life. This encouraged them to focus on the present, avoiding the traps of both past regret and future anxiety—a mindset that can help curtail the spiraling anxieties bred on social media platforms.

2.6. Stoicism Today

In today's world, the relevance of Stoicism isn't confined to individual peace of mind. It extends to building resilient societies, capable of withstanding hardships. When we adopt Stoic principles, we don't just better our own lives; our enhanced perspective can positively impact our interactions with others, reverberating throughout our social networks—online and off.

Guided by virtues and wisdom, we can navigate the confusing terrains of social media, upholding fairness, patience, and resilience. The Stoic doesn't shun the digital world, but learns to engage with it in a healthier, more fulfilling manner, illuminating the virtual world with ancient wisdom reinvented for the modern age.

Now equipped with a deeper understanding of Stoicism, let's delve into the specifics of how we can apply these principles to our daily social media interactions, fortifying our mental resilience and bringing tranquility to our digital activities.

Chapter 3. The Social Media Landscape: Navigating the Chaos

Before venturing into the vast and intricate landscape of social media, it would help to have a map or a guidebook—a handy instrument that acquaints you with the terrain, the inhabitants, the opportunities, and, of course, the potential pitfalls. Think of this chapter as your 'virtual compass,' designed to help you approach social media with an informed and balanced perspective. This isn't about retreating from the digital world but about charting a course that enables serenity amidst the chaos.

3.1. Understanding the Terrain of Social Media

The terrain of social media could be likened to an interlinked set of dynamic, bustling towns, each representing different platforms such as Facebook, Instagram, Twitter, LinkedIn, etc. These 'towns' are culturally distinct, inhabited by diverse crowds and governed by their unique sets of rules. Facebook might strike you as a sprawling metropolis, buzzing with family and friends, news, events, and a staggering array of groups and discussions. Twitter is the global town square, where conversations—ranging from the mundane to the revolutionary—unfurl in real time. Instagram is like a vibrant arts and culture hub where aesthetics reign supreme. LinkedIn, being the corporate town, pulsates with professional networking, job opportunities, and industry insights. Understanding these different landscapes forms the ground zero of navigating the chaos.

3.2. Acknowledging the Impact

To navigate effectively and healthily, one must not only acquaint themselves with the terrain of social media but also acknowledge its profound influence. Remember the ancient Stoic axiom to "change what is within our control and accept what is not"? Despite its virtual nature, social media's impact on our perceptions, emotions, and experiences is very real—making it an external factor that we must accept and contend with. It can create social comparison, foster the 'fear of missing out' (FOMO), and even strain mental health. However, it's also a tool for learning, connecting, and advocating for causes. Recognize this dual-nature of social media—it will serve as your North Star when the seas get stormy.

3.3. Cultivating Stoic Armor for Your Mind

At the heart of our approach is the cultivation of a "Stoic Armor"—a mental buffer that allows you to engage with social media while maintaining emotional equilibrium. Embracing Marcus Aurelius' idea that "You have power over your mind, not outside events," you can control how you interact with social media. Don't let a negative comment or controversial post upset your tranquility.

Mainstays of this armor are self-awareness, discretion, and mindfulness. Know your emotional triggers, what makes you anxious or upset. Before reacting to a post, take a moment to reflect: Is it necessary to engage? Will it contribute positively? Online interactions can be a mirror of your mental state—by maintaining mindfulness, you're not simply a reactive entity but an active participant who choses their battles wisely.

3.4. Identifying Emotional Pitfalls

Just as a travel guide warns you about dangerous terrains or hostile inhabitants, this chapter highlights the common emotional pitfalls encountered in the social media landscape—trolling, cyberbullying, echo chambers, and information overload.

Trolling and cyberbullying are increasingly common phenomena that could affect your mental well-being. Here, remember the words of the great Stoic philosopher Epictetus, "It's not what happens to you, but how you react to it that matters." Instead of retaliating or withdrawing, respond wisely or disconnect when necessary.

Echo chambers and filter bubbles can narrow your perspective, amplify biases, and even propagate false information. Remember the tenets of stoicism: perceive clearly, think critically, and remain open to alternative viewpoints. Information overload can lead to anxiety or confusion—practice digital minimalism to cope with this. Handpick your sources of information and define specific social media times to maintain balance.

3.5. Curating Your Virtual Oasis

Think about curating your social media platforms to create what we'd like to refer to as a 'Virtual Oasis'—a space for growth, serenity, and meaningful connection. Follow accounts, groups, or channels that offer value, inspire positivity, and promote a balanced perspective. Contribute meaningfully to discussions, advocate for causes you believe in, and connect with like-minded individuals. Create content that reflects your authentic self, not a perfectly curated persona.

A Stoic view encourages you to realize the potential and the limitations of social media. While it provides the tools to charter your navigation through online chaos, the responsibility remains yours to stay tranquil and steady. It's about accepting the external tumult and recognizing that true power rests in your response to the chaos.

Chapter 4. Stoicism and Social Media: The Unexpected Synergy

In today's digital age, social media is an unbelievable force. There are valuable connections to be made, insights to be gleaned, and a global conversation to partake in. However, as much as this virtual environment can foster growth, it can also trigger stress, anxiety, and self-doubt. How can a 2000-year-old philosophy help guide us through this wilderness? Let's dive in.

4.1. The Framework of Stoicism

Stoicism, the ancient philosophy founded in Athens by Zeno of Citium in the early 3rd century BC, teaches us to manage our reactions to the world around us. Although we may not fully control everything that happens, we have complete authority over how we respond.

Stoics classify everything into two categories: Things within our control (our beliefs, our actions, and our reactions) and things outside our control (events, other people, the past and future). Recognizing this can liberate us from the psychological burden the uncontrollable elements in life often impose.

How does this relate to the chaos of social media? The online world, with its influx of information and opinions, is largely outside of our control. As Stoics, we must refocus our energy not on controlling the uncontrollable, but on controlling our responses.

4.2. Embracing Dichotomy of Control Online

Our reactions to social media, be it likes, comments, or shares, are well within our control. Instead of anxiously pondering about how many likes your post will receive—which tallies into the uncontrollable—we can focus on creating content that aligns with our values and beliefs, which is within our control.

Accepting this online dichotomy of control liberates us from feeling personally rejected or insufficient when our posts don't attract the expected engagement. Conversely, it prevents us from becoming overly elated or prideful upon receiving excessive praise. Stoicism is the steadying hand on the tiller of our emotional ship, keeping us balanced and composed in the turbulent social media seas.

4.3. The Stoic's Code: Virtue is the Sole Good

Stoics firmly believe that virtue is the highest good. They identify four cardinal virtues: wisdom, courage, justice, and temperance. How do these virtues translate in our virtual life?

Wisdom is recognizing what's within our control and choosing how to best use that control. It's about creating thoughtful, meaningful content and understanding when to disconnect to prevent overconsumption or cyberbullying.

Courage relates to asserting your beliefs and values online despite potential opposition. It's about choosing not to engage in toxic dialogues and rising above online harassment.

Justice is recognizing the importance of fairness and equality in all interactions and sharing content that highlights these values. It's about using social media platforms as a force for good, voicing support for marginalized groups, or advocating for societal change.

Temperance, the virtue of moderation, keeps us from becoming consumed by the virtual world. It involves setting boundaries to ensure that our online lives don't derail our real lives.

By grounding your social media interactions with these virtues, you can create a meaningful and positive online presence.

4.4. News and Stoic Indifference

While social media brings us global news at our fingertips, it also exposes us to distressing reports that can affect our emotional state. Here, Stoic indifference can guide us.

Stoic indifference doesn't mean total lack of concern. It refers to a calm, composed perspective, free from excess emotional turmoil. It enables us to witness tragedy or injustice and maintain a balanced state of mind to plan an effective response.

By applying stoic indifference, we can engage with the suffering world through social media, empathize, and mobilize, without becoming emotionally drained.

4.5. Maintaining Marshmallow Resilience

The chaotic environment of social media can be draining. However, the Stoic concept of 'marshmallow resilience' provides a robust defence. It's about collecting tiny bits of resilience—like a marshmallow collecting snowflakes—that accumulate into a formidable bulwark.

Microresilience techniques include the practice of amor fati—the love of fate—and memento mori—awareness of mortality. Each time you are stressed due to an online incident, remember amor fati and accept the situation. Each time you waste hours aimlessly scrolling, remember memento mori and make your finite time count. These small acts enhance your overall resilience.

4.6. Wrapping Up

The wisdom of Stoicism aids us in navigating the often tumultuous world of social media. This philosophy invites us to question our online behaviors, refocus our energy on aspects within our control, and cultivate virtues that uphold our mental tranquility. By combining the age-old wisdom with our daily digital lives, we find an unexpected synergy, helping us not just survive, but thrive amidst the online chaos.

Chapter 5. Building Mental Resilience: A Stoic's Approach

Welcome! You are stepping into the journey of thriving—rather than merely surviving—in the tumultuous realm of virtual interaction. It begins with a consistent and robust approach to developing mental resilience; an approach steeped in a philosophy that has withstood the test of time. Let us embark on a comprehensive exploration of how to build that strength using Stoic philosophy.

5.1. Understanding Stoicism

Stoicism originates from ancient Greece and Rome, boasting illustrious proponents like Seneca, Epictetus, and Marcus Aurelius. At its core, Stoicism is about understanding and accepting the dichotomy of control in life, advocating that one can achieve tranquility and resilience by focusing only on what one can control: our own judgments, impulses, desires, and aversions. By doing so, we remain untouched and serene amidst external chaos and turmoil – a state of mind we crave when navigating the tumultuous seas of social media.

5.2. Dichotomy of Control in Social Media

In the context of social media, understanding the dichotomy of control helps us discern what we can and cannot influence. Despite appearances, the content and behavior of others—opinions, comments, posts—are beyond our direct control. Therefore, per the dichotomy principle, our energy must pivot towards our responses and our attitudes towards these instances. Sobriety in thought and action fosters emotional calmness and resilience as we engage online.

5.3. Observing Without Judging

Given the abundance of information and perspectives found online, it is easy to react hastily and emotionally. Stoicism proposes an alternative: observing without immediate judgement. This involves processing information objectively, without allowing personal biases or emotions to intervene, and inevitably leads to a more thoughtful and measured response. The key is to practice restraint in our mind before we manifest it in our behavior.

5.4. Cultivating Inner Tranquility

Being consistently unaffected by the uproar on social media requires inner tranquility. To achieve this, regularly reminding ourselves of the ephemerality of most online content can be helpful. An offensive tweet, a controversial post, or an online disagreement—most are fleeting and inconsequential in the grand canvas of life. Put into context, it is easier to maintain equanimity.

5.5. Reevaluating Desires and Aversions

A primary source of disruption in our social media experience is triggered by our specific desires and aversions. For instance, the desire for online validation and fear of critique can make social media a very stressful landscape to navigate. To mitigate this, Stoicism encourages us to critically evaluate our desires and fears. Are likes, comments, and followers supremely important? Or is there greater value in using social media platforms as tools for learning, connection, and positive impact? A shift in this orientation equips us with a resilient mindset.

5.6. Embracing a Stoic Perspective on Social Interactions

A Stoic views social interactions as opportunities for practicing virtues like justice, kindness, and understanding. Applying this to our digital footprints promotes healthier dialogue and improves both our own and possibly others' mental well-being. That offensive comment might just become an opportunity to showcase understanding and patience.

5.7. Emotional Preparedness: Expectation Management

Expecting perfection from ourselves or others only breeds stress and disappointment, especially online. Instead, Stoicism advises that we recognize the imperfections in ourselves and others, allowing us to manage our expectations better. When paired with the practice of premeditatio malorum (foreseeing things that could go wrong), we equip ourselves with emotional armor that shields against the unpredictability of online interactions.

5.8. Skepticism as a Stoic Tool

The stoics were wise skeptics, questioning everything before accepting or dismissing it. Given the spread of misinformation and bias online, we too must incorporate skepticism into our social media use. This healthy suspicion encourages us to critically assess information and prevents us from falling prey to false or misleading content.

5.9. The Stoic Practice of Askesis

Askesis, a practice of routine self-discipline and introspection, is a valuable strategy to hone mental resilience. Incorporating habits like regular digital detoxes, time-bound social media usage, and constant evaluation of our online interactions can exert positive change in our digital lives.

5.10. The Last Word: Amor Fati

Amor Fati, or "love of fate," is the Stoic practice of accepting and embracing whatever life throws at us. Translate this to our social media engagement as unconditional acceptance of the ups and downs of the virtual world, maintaining our tranquility, and continuing to learn and grow throughout it all.

Implementing these strategies guarantees not a perfect, but healthier, more satisfying, online experience. It allows us to build on our mental resilience and thrive amidst the chaos and unpredictability inherent in social media. Immerse yourself in this journey of transformation, and empower yourself to not just survive, but flourish in the Digital Age.

Chapter 6. The Art of Not Being Affected: Achieving Digital Detachment

It is a well-observed reality that in this age of digital connectivity and constant social buzz, detachment from our devices might seem not only challenging but nearly impossible. However, adopting stoic principles can help us navigate these online waters, curate a peaceful state of mind and avoid unhelpful distractions or emotional drains.

6.1. Breathing Space from the Instant Gratification Habit

The immediate nature of digital communication becomes a reflex – post a photo, check the likes, put out a tweet, count the retweets. It's a cycle we often find ourselves trapped in. As the alarm bell rings — a notification, an emoji, words in bold — we rush to engage, fearing we might miss out.

A stoic approach to this would involve slowing down those responses. Teach yourself to resist the urge to open the app multiple times a day. Allow yourself to not know, to let the likes accumulate while you focus on a non-digital task. Reclaim control over your digital interactions by focusing on the task at hand. Constantly remind yourself that social media should be only one of many facets of your life, and that real life exists outside the digital realm, requiring your attention and energy.

6.2. Strengthening Emotional Resilience

Practicing Stoics acknowledge that not all events are within their control, but how they react is. When it comes to social media, there's a lot that's beyond our power: What someone posts, the content we are exposed to, and even the platform's guiding algorithms. Consequently, our reactions need to be detached, thoughtful, and measured.

When you encounter a post that upsets you, pause. Reflect consciously on your emotional response. Understand that each person's perspective is shaped by their unique experiences, and their content doesn't necessarily reflect universal truth. Choosing to disengage or responding calmly can save you from unnecessary emotional turmoil.

Take on the stoic practice of reflecting on your emotional responses. By being more self-aware, you cultivate emotional resilience and, in turn, become far less susceptible to negative emotions triggered by social media content.

6.3. The Shift from Comparison to Self-Reflection

Social media has an inescapable element of comparison. However, comparison, as per stoic philosophy, can lead to dissatisfaction and discontent. Stoics believe in self-reflection, stating that our main competitor is our past selves. When it comes to social media, this perspective can be a game-changer.

Every time you catch yourself comparing your life to those highlight reals, gently guide your thoughts towards your own progress. Are you evolving from the person you were yesterday? Do you see growth, change, learning? This shift from comparison to self-reflection can be profoundly liberating.

6.4. Making Intentional Choices on Social Media

Being a stoic involves making conscious, mindful choices about one's actions. On social media, this means mindfully deciding what to share, what to view, and how to interact. Avoid impulse posting or commenting, instead taking a moment to assess its value and potential impact.

A stoic is also aware of the transience of all things, including social media trends. Resist the pull to follow all trends or constantly stay updated. Choose to engage with those that align with your beliefs, interests, or hobbies. When you choose intentional interactions on social media, you pave the way for healthier online relationships and use the medium for personal growth and positivity.

6.5. Unplugging and Reconnecting — Offline

The most concrete step towards digital detachment is a physical separation from our devices every now and then. A 'Digital Detox', as it's commonly known today, comes highly recommended. Even if for a short while, unplugging allows us the space to reconnect with our offline realities. It grants us the opportunity to indulge in activities that contribute to our overall well-being and inner peace.

By training ourselves to detach, we are implicitly deciding not to be dictated by the ebb and flow of the virtual world. Applying stoicism in this context allows us to retain control over our thoughts, our time, and eventually our life, even in the midst of growing digital chaos.

6.6. Concluding Remarks

Emulating the stoics might initially seem demanding in a digital world, but the reward in the form of peace, control, and resilience is worth the effort. The internet need not be a battlefield fraught with anxiety. With these tools in hand, we can traverse it with serenity and strength.

Remember, it's not necessary to severe all digital ties; the aim is to build a healthier relationship with the virtual space. One where we are not perturbed by a barrage of tweets or posts but can stand as a stoic beacon, shining light on how to navigate the digital landscape with grace and tranquility.

Chapter 7. Perception and Reaction: The Key Concepts of Online Stoicism

Understanding the world of social media can sometimes feel like untangling the Gordian Knot. In order to navigate this intricate labyrinth with grace, we must first comprehend two core concepts: perception and reaction.

The ancient Stoics—philosophers who roamed the streets of Athens and Rome—held that our perception of events, rather than the events themselves, defines our experience. They firmly believed in distinguishing between what we can control and what we can't. In other words, we can't control the actions, words, or the posts of others, but we can control our own perception and reaction to them.

7.1. Perception: Your Lens to the Digital World

Stoicism teaches us that our perceptions can alter our reality. On social media platforms, this concept cuts through the chaos like a beam of clarity. Each post we encounter on our screens is like a seed; our perception, the soil in which it plants itself. It is our perception that determines whether this seed grows into a lush or a toxic plant.

However, the limitless stream of information consumes us, stirring potent whirlwinds of news, opinions, and advertisements. Sentiments like fear, anger, and joy emanate from this chaos, often clouding our perception. Social media designs can accentuate our most impulsive, reactive tendencies, as they strive to keep us scrolling, clicking, and engaging.

So, the challenge lies not in the platform itself or the people using it. These are things we can't control. Instead, the challenge is maintaining a reasonable and composed perception amidst the cacophony. Practicing Stoicism suggests sifting through this noise, impartially observing each social media storm, and calmly appointing meaning to the posts and comments we encounter. This process of mindful perception, of viewing through a stoic lens, is the first step to peacefully navigating social media platforms.

7.2. Reaction: Your Power in the Digital World

A reactive mind often acts as a puppet on social media strings. A comment can incite anger, a post can plunge us into sadness. Through the dust of swirling emotions, it can feel as if external factors on social media have a stranglehold on our state of mind. Stoicism teaches us to dissolve this illusion and uncover the inherent power we have over our reactions.

Closely tied with perception, our reaction in the stoic realm is a realm we rule with complete sovereignty. It is our conscious response to our perception. Upon encountering negativity on social media, we can opt for distress, or we can perceive it as a part of the world's inherent nature—neither good nor bad, just existent.

For this, Marcus Aurelius, the Stoic Roman Emperor, guides us with his wisdom, "You have power over your mind—not outside events. Realize this, and you will find strength." When scrolling through social media posts, remember, you have the power to choose—to engage, ignore, or respond with kindness. No matter how disruptive a tweet or post may seem, our reaction can always be our sanctuary of tranquility and reason.

7.3. Transforming Perception and Reaction: Practical Steps

Armed with these two powerful tools, perception and reaction, let's step into practical realm. Below we outline a series of small, manageable steps that can render your social media experience one imbued with stoic wisdom.

1. Listen to your emotional response, but don't let it control you.
2. Practice the '\pause and respond' mantra rather than the 'react impulsively' approach.
3. Use every offense or conflict as an opportunity to build mental resilience.
4. Regularly spend a few moments engaging with positive, comforting content.

Remember, these steps are not a rigid prescription, rather gentle guidance towards tranquility and composure.

7.4. Building a Stoic Routine on Social Media

Abstract as they sound, the principles of Stoicism can be incorporated into our daily routines for a healthier social media life.

For instance, start by dedicating five minutes each day to observe your emotional reactions on social media without engaging. With time, extend this practice, achieving eventual mastery over your digital reactions. Curate your social media feed to enrich it with content that sparks positivity, joy, and inspiration. Over time, these small changes can transform your entire relationship with social media platforms.

This dynamic interplay between perception and reaction is the Stoic's lens through which we navigate the accelerating digital world. Understanding and implementing these principles doesn't just equip you to face social media—it empowers you to thrive amidst the chaos, with unflinching wisdom and composure. In the end, it's not about controlling the digital world around us, but nurturing the Stoic inside us.

Chapter 8. Managing Online Relationships: A Stoicism-Inspired Guide

Before we embark on the intricacies of managing online relationships through the lens of Stoicism, it's worth taking a moment to recall the core tenets of Stoic philosophy. Three fundamental principles are control, acceptance, and detachment—and we'll explore how integrating these into your online behavior can drastically reshape your virtual relationships.

8.1. Understanding What is Under Your Control

Stoic philosophy emphasizes understanding the dichotomy of control. Clearly categorizing matters into 'things you can control' and 'things you cannot control' alleviates unnecessary stress and provides clarity in interactions. This principle applies equally to your online existence.

When it comes to social media, decipher what is under your control. Your posts, comments, reactions, and the people or pages you choose to follow are entirely under your control. You have the power to express yourself and define who you engage with.

On the other hand, others' posts, comments, and the number of likes or followers you garner are beyond your control. They are products of other people's judgments, decisions, and algorithms, all of which lie outside your realm of influence.

Start exercising control where you can. Scrutinize the people and pages you follow and ensure they contribute positively to your online experience. Dedicate time to curate your digital environment and fill it with motivation, knowledge, and positivity. Remember, timing as well is under your control. Regulate when you interact with your device and how long you spend in the digital realm.

8.2. Distinguishing Between Opinion and Fact

Social media is an echo chamber where varied opinions masquerade as facts. Here, the Stoic tool of critical analysis comes to the rescue. Question the source of information and the reality of situations. Understand that every statement on social media is a representation of an individual's perspective and prejudiceds, and doesn't necessarily reflect the truth. Distinguishing facts from opinions guards against misinformation and promotes well-informed online relationships.

8.3. Embracing Acceptance

Stoicism teaches acceptance of things that are beyond our control. This acceptance is the key to maintaining sanity in the buzz of likes, tweets, posts, and shares. Learn to accept the nature of social media—its simultaneity of disagreement and agreement, positivity and negativity, truth and falsehood. Don't forget, the number of likes, shares, or retweets is a poor metric for self-worth. Treat them objectively, for what they are: a reflection of others' preferences, not your value.

8.4. Harnessing Emotional Detachment

The capacity to separate ourselves from phenomena that we have no control over is the heart of emotional detachment. A mean comment, an insensitive post—these don't have to turn your day upside down. Remind yourself of the opinions-facts discernment and maintain perspective. Allow people to have their viewpoints without allowing it to affect your state of mind.

8.5. Building an Oasis of Positivity

Nurture your social media platforms as an oasis of positivity. Share uplifting content and create a space of light-heartedness and constructive thought. Building such an environment not only enhances your own experience but may also serve as a beacon for others lost in the chaos.

8.6. Fostering Depth in Relationships

Look beyond the screens and cultivate depth in relationships. Use social media as a stepping stone to engage in deeper, more meaningful conversations. Reach out, listen, share experiences, and foster empathy.

8.7. Conclusion

To successfully manage online relationships, we must remember to distinguish between what we can control and what we cannot, to sift facts from opinions, accept the imperfections of the virtual world, remain emotionally detached from the fluctuations of online activity, create a positive digital environment, and above all, cultivate genuine relationships. Just as the ancient Stoics found tranquillity amidst the bustle of ancient Rome, we too can find tranquillity amidst the buzz of the digital age. Steady yourself and begin to surf the wave!

Chapter 9. Redefining Digital Success: Stoic Principles in Action

Social media, while it has revolutionized the way we communicate, can often feel like a whirlwind of emotions, information, and distractions. Constantly measuring our value based on likes, shares, and follower counts can be draining. This whirlwind, however, isn't the result of the technology itself, but an outcome of our responses and behaviors. What if we redefine the metrics for success? Stoicism, an ancient philosophy of enduring pain or adversity with perseverance, places great emphasis on accepting only those things under our control and developing indifference to the rest.

9.1. Practising Inner Disjunction

Inner disjunction may sound intricate, but it's essentially the application of the Stoic idea that our reason perceives the world, not the world itself. Events, posts, comments, and the like are simply sensations that we interpret. A negative comment on your post may appear hurtful, but it doesn't have to be. The hurt isn't in the comment, but in our interpretation of it. This way, we start to gain immunity against the chaotic exterior by forming a calm interior.

9.2. Act Not React: The Stoic Approach to Online Engagement

As we actively engage on social media platforms, Stoics encourage us to act and not react. And there's a big difference. Acting involves conscious decision-making based on our values, principles, and an understanding of the situation. Reacting, on the other hand, is an impulsive response usually driven by our emotions. When we act, we maintain our tranquility and composure, and also our dignity.

9.3. Thriving Through Virtue: Real Social Media Goals

In Stoicism, virtue is the highest good—a summation of wisdom, courage, justice, and moderation. When we redefine our digital success in terms of these virtues, we no longer rely on fleeting statuses such as likes or shares. It's about how many lives we can positively impact through our content, how courageously we can stand against injustice, how wisely we share our insights, and how balanced we keep our virtual and real lives.

9.4. Stoic Mindfulness: Present, Attentive, Fulfilled

Given the sensory overload social media sometimes offers, the Stoic practice of mindfulness teaches us to stay present and attentive. Rather than mindlessly scrolling through our feed, we curate the information we consume, engage in insightful conversations, and, most importantly, know when to log off. This doesn't just keep our mind healthier but also makes our time spent more fulfilling.

9.5. Managing Fear of Missing Out (FOMO)

One of the leading causes of stress and unhappiness related to social media is the FOMO. Stoicism helps cope with this modern phenomenon by encouraging us to appreciate what we have and where we are. FOMO subsides when we start focusing on personal growth, meaningful interactions, and cultivating gratitude for the small joys in our life.

9.6. Rethinking Negative Emotions: Ways to Triumph Over Trolls

As in real life, our digital life isn't immune to negative situations or people. A Stoic lens helps here too. In the face of harmful comments or trolling, Stoics advise us to separate the action from the person. To acknowledge that, in most cases, people who indulge in such behavior are themselves in turmoil. This doesn't excuse poor behavior, but provides a compassionate framework to approach such situations.

9.7. The Wisdom of Unplugging: Seeking Virtue Offscreen

While this guide focuses on navigating the tumultuous seas of social media, the Stoics would likely remind us that the offline world deserves equal, if not more, attention. No matter how harmonious our online interaction becomes, it's pivotal to maintain relationships, hobbies, and interests offscreen.

Learning to apply these Stoic principles to your online behaviors will not only inoculate you against the occasional storms of social media, but it can also make your journey through the digital world inspiring, nurturing and enriching. Redefining success isn't just about changing how we perceive likes and shares; it's about transforming our online existence to serve a deeper, more meaningful purpose.

Chapter 10. Combating Cyberbullying: The Stoic's Shield

In the tumultuous virtual world where opinions are expressed freely and reactions emerge rapidly, it's a reality that the ghostly specter of cyberbullying lingers. This digital incarnation of traditional bullying can be an insidious and pervasive source of distress. However, considering the lens of Stoicism offers a profound, yet practical suite of strategies to combat this modern scourge. This ancient philosophy teaches us that while we cannot control external occurrences, we can certainly control our reaction to them. That's our focus here as we steer a course through the disarray, armed with wisdom dating back to Marcus Aurelius and Epictetus.

10.1. Setting The Stage: Understanding Cyberbullying

Cyberbullying constitutes any aggressive, intentional act performed repeatedly over digital platforms against a victim who can't easily defend themselves. It involves harmful material sent online or posted publicly intended to cause distress. To combat it, we first need to understand it.

1. **Recognition:** Identify the various forms it can take, such as sending offensive messages, spreading rumors, sharing intimate images or content out-of-context, or creating harmful websites.

2. **Reaction:** Understand how it affects the person being targeted. Effects can be deeply psychological; lowered confidence, increased anxiety, depression, or even suicidal thoughts.

3. **Response:** Define your personal protocol in such situations. Who

should you alert (friends, family, site administrators, professionals)? What action can you take against the bully (blocking, reporting, legal action)?

Keeping these points in mind, you become better equipped to handle the situation when it arises.

10.2. Stoicism Basics: Control, Endurance, and Perspective

Stoicism posits two realms: the external, which we cannot control (events, other people's actions, the weather) and internal, which we can control (our actions, reactions, beliefs). This dichotomy of control is one of the most powerful tools in a stoic's arsenal.

The second key stoic principle is endurance, which isn't about gritting your teeth and suffering in silence—it's about transforming obstacles into opportunities.

Thirdly, perspective. How we perceive a situation drastically influences our emotional responses. It's important to remind ourselves that perception is something we can control.

10.3. Building The Shield: The Stoic's Approach to Combat Cyberbullying

Armed with these stoic principles, we can create a shield of resilience against cyberbullying.

1. **Control Your Reaction:** Emphasize your sphere of control—most importantly, your responses. While you cannot control someone's intent to harm, you can control your reaction to their actions. Cyberbullies seek negative reactions; don't feed them emotional responses. Stay calm, and respond—if you choose

to—dispassionately, focusing on the logic of the situation.

2. **Perseverance:** Bullying is a trial, but every trial offers an opportunity for growth. This isn't an invitation to accept the situation passively, but rather to actively confront it by asserting your right to a safe digital space and standing up for others if they are targeted.

3. **Perspective:** Try to view the situation objectively. Could the bully's actions reflect their struggles and insecurities? That isn't to excuse their behavior, but it can dilute its sting, particularly if you realise that the issue lies with them, not with you.

10.4. Becoming the "Point at Which the Universe is Taking Its Footing"

Epictetus once said that the stoic sage acts as the "point at which the universe is taking its footing," grounding themselves steadfastly amidst the chaos. Today, this could be seen as becoming a source of positivity and support in your online community, offering a safe haven amidst the whirlwind of negativity that can characterize online interactions. Set an example to others through your actions and responses. This is where the fight against cyberbullying becomes a collective effort.

10.5. The Aftermath: Dealing with Hurt and Damage

Acknowledging that you're hurt doesn't make you weak. Stoic philosophy embraces feeling but cautions against being governed by it. Seek help when needed, and don't hesitate to involve mentors, counselors, and authorities in serious cases.

To sum up, the stoic approach to combating cyberbullying involves fostering individual resilience, nurturing healthier online communities, and promoting strength and dignity in the face of adversity. It is about not just surviving, but thriving in your virtual life, navigating the chaos and maelstrom with composure and tranquility.

Remember, Marcus Aurelius once noted, "You have power over your mind — not outside events. Realize this, and you will find strength." Use this strength to build your shield against cyberbullying. The online world can be a limitless, rewarding realm if navigated with the right perspective, serene tenacity, and quiet dignity that Stoicism fosters.

Chapter 11. Maintaining Digital Wellness: A Stoic's Habitual Routine

Before delving into the strategies and practices that will form your Stoic habitual routine in maintaining digital wellness, it's crucial to understand why it's essential. The constant stream of information, news, opinions, and digital chatter we interact with daily can significantly influence our emotional state, thought processes and even our perception of reality. Navigating this digital landscape with a Stoic mindset provides us the tools needed to maintain our mental equilibrium amidst the noise.

11.1. Attaining Digital Equanimity

Marcus Aurelius, a notable Stoic philosopher, declared, "If you are distressed by anything external, the pain is not due to the thing itself but to your estimate of it; and this you have the power to revoke at any moment." This principle holds in the digital world too.

To maintain digital wellness, create a regular practice of centering yourself. Find a calm inner place where you are not affected by digital turmoil. Treat likes, dislikes, comments, or shares unemotionally. Respond objectively to trolls or cyberbullying without letting it impact your inner tranquility.

Creating such a calming ritual could involve methods like quietly sipping morning tea while keeping devices turned off, setting particular times for checking social media, or keeping some time for digital detox within a day. Make these rituals part of your everyday routines. Gradually you would notice a substantial shift in your digital interactions. They become less chaotic and taxing as you learn to stay absorbed in your inner tranquility, undisturbed by the maelstrom of the internet.

11.2. Identifying and Controlling Cognitive Distortions

Cognitive distortions are irrational or exaggerated thought patterns that can sway our feelings and actions. On social media, irrational thoughts can be triggered easily due to constant exposure to negative news feeds, polarized debates, or unrealistic lifestyle images. Stoicism teaches us to be aware of and control such distorted reactions.

Stoic philosopher Epictetus stated, "People are disturbed not by things, but by the views they take of them." While deliberating on any social media update, focus on realities and not your emotional interpretation of them. It's crucial to spot and question cognitive distortions. This will significantly decrease the likelihood of experiencing negative emotions like anxiety, jealousy, or anger arising from distorted thoughts.

It's useful to follow a Stoic 'detachment' exercise. Take a step back from your immediate reaction to a social media update, understand it neutrally, reflect on the emotion it triggered, and then respond objectively. It's not about being emotionless, but about steering your emotions and controlling their impact on you.

11.3. Practicing Meaningful Engagements

The stoic approach promotes purposeful and value-adding interactions over mindless scrolling or counterproductive debates. A Stoic would advise you to ask yourself, "Is this adding value to my life or the lives of others?" before partaking in any digital interaction.

Set meaningful personal goals related to your online behavior. Reduce time spent on vain browsing or irrelevant engagements. Focus on purposeful information or communities that encourage learning or constructive discussions. This practice not only directs your digital activity towards growth but also helps in decluttering the inundation of trivial digital info.

11.4. Embracing Digital Minimalism

"Make the best use of what is in your power, and review the rest as it happens," stated Epictetus. This references not only events in life but also your digital engagements.

Embrace digital minimalism by reviewing and limiting the apps, notifications, email subscriptions, podcasts, and platforms you engage in. Following a strategy of 'less is more' lets you retain control over your digital life, curbs information overload, and unlocks time and mental space for meaningful endeavors.

To conclude, attaining digital wellness involves a medley of understanding the harmful elements of social media, strong mental practices, and proactive steps to structure your digital activities. A regular Stoic routine comprising of the practices suggested above can equip you with the tools to not just survive but thrive in the world of social media. Remember, adopting such habits would not happen overnight. Progress would be slow and gradual. Remain patient and consistent. The key is to commit to the journey towards achieving a robust mental resilience against the online chaos. Let your voyage through the digital world be governed by the timeless wisdom of Stoicism for a healthier and happier virtual life.

www.ingramcontent.com/pod-product-compliance
Lightning Source LLC
Chambersburg PA
CBHW060855260726
48661CB00008B/3286